For Ash, who gives me courage.
And for Christopher and Ellie, my two favorite monsters.

©2023 Family Fables LLC

All rights reserved, including the right to reproduce this book or portions thereof in any form whatsoever.
First Edition
ISBN-13: 978-1-951173-22-7

For information about authoring or illustrating your own children's book, visit www.familyfables.org.

BRIAN THE GHOST

A FAMILY FABLE

Story by: Chris Dugovich

Art by: Tanya Berezovskaya

Brian just wanted to read **BOOKS**, and play **GAMES**, and watch **MOVIES**. But more than anything, BRIAN wanted a **REAL-LIFE FRIEND**.

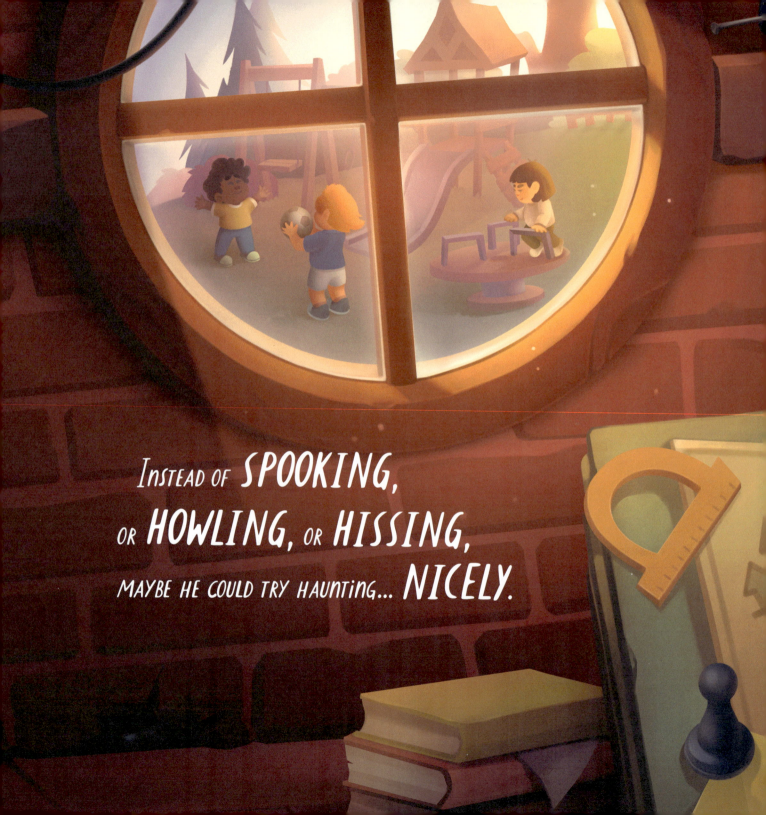

Instead of SPOOKING, or HOWLING, or HISSING, maybe he could try haunting... NICELY.

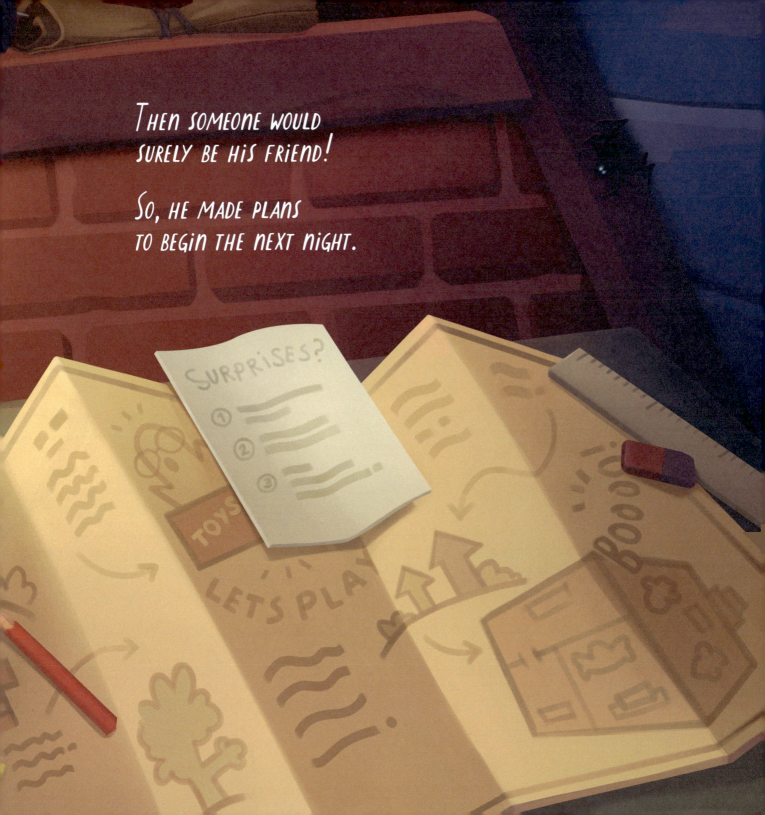

The first night, Brian went to the **BLEECKER** house.

So, on the third night, he went to the SMITH'S, where the family was cozied up in front of the television.

And Brian did not want to be scary.
He just wanted to be Brian.
Perfectly normal, regular, everyday Brian.

And he still very much wanted a friend.

So, the two new friends laughed and played late into the night in the quiet — well, maybe not so quiet — town of St. Germaine.

Made in United States
Troutdale, OR
09/29/2023